MOVING BEYOND MYTHS

Revitalizing Undergraduate Mathematics

Committee on the Mathematical Sciences
in the Year 2000

Board on Mathematical Sciences

Mathematical Sciences Education Board

National Research Council

NATIONAL ACADEMY PRESS
Washington, D.C.
1991

NATIONAL ACADEMY PRESS • 2101 Constitution Avenue, N.W. • Washington, D.C. 20418

Support for this project and for the publication and dissemination of the report was provided by grants from the National Science Foundation and the National Security Agency with additional support from the Department of Education and the National Aeronautics and Space Administration.

Cover photograph reprinted courtesy of the University of Maryland and with permission from John Consoli, photographer. Copyright © 1989 by John Consoli.

FOREWORD

Anyone who believes that educational reform is something needed only at the school level will be disabused of that notion by reading *Moving Beyond Myths: Revitalizing Undergraduate Mathematics*. This report, prepared by a committee of 20 distinguished citizens from academia, industry, and public policy, calls for sweeping change in mathematics education at the college-university level to parallel change underway in the nation's schools, noting that both levels play key roles in advancing science and technology and in preparing the broader work force and quantitatively literate citizenry the country needs.

The publication of *Moving Beyond Myths* completes a decade of effort in which boards and committees of the National Research Council have analyzed the total U.S. mathematical sciences enterprise. This unique undertaking begin in 1981 with the appointment of the so-called David committee, which in 1984 published its review of the status of U.S. mathematical research, along with a national plan for renewal; an update, *Renewing U.S. Mathematics: A Plan for the 1990s*, was published last year. In 1989, *Everybody Counts — A Report to the Nation on the Future of Mathematics Education* presented an overall assessment of the quality and status of mathematics education, outlining a strategy and plan for reforming school mathematics. As 1991 begins, we have the capstone, *Moving Beyond Myths*, which puts forth a similar plan for college-university mathematics, a plan designed to fit with those found in *Everybody Counts* and *Renewing U.S. Mathematics*. All of these three-year reviews were undertaken at the request of the U.S. mathematics and mathematics education communities, but were conducted by NRC committees representing the diverse constituencies of the mathematical sciences.

The Committee on the Mathematical Sciences in the Year 2000 has been ably led by Dr. William E. Kirwan, President of the University of Maryland at College Park, since the time in 1989 when other pressing commitments drew away the first chair, Mr. J. Fred Bucy, former Chief Executive Officer of Texas Instruments, Inc.

The MS2000 Committee's report presents a formidable challenge to higher education, especially to the nation's research universities. I urge all who read *Moving Beyond Myths* to reflect on it in the context of the other major reports I have mentioned and to identify their roles in implementing the action plan it contains.

Frank Press
President, National Academy of Sciences
Chairman, National Research Council

PREFACE

The national action plan presented in *Moving Beyond Myths: Revitalizing Undergraduate Mathematics* calls for dramatic change. Its implementation will tax the creativity, commitment, adaptability, and energies of mathematical sciences faculty and departments, college-university administrations and trustees, professional societies, and federal and state governments. Success will depend upon the cooperation of all these groups in a sustained effort lasting to the year 2000 and beyond. The plan challenges our institutions of higher education to bring their mathematics education efforts up to the standard set by the nation's mathematical research enterprise, which is preeminent in the world.

The President and the governors of the 50 states have set just such a standard of performance by U.S. schools, colleges, and universities as a national goal for mathematics and science education. Our report states what we think it will take for undergraduate mathematics to reach this ambitious goal.

The challenge is reminiscent of the one faced by the nation's universities at the middle of this century: To develop the infrastructure necessary to support scientific research of the highest quality. The response to that pressing national need was a post-World War II cooperative effort of the universities and government that produced the greatest scientific research enterprise in history, built upon a new kind of institution: the modern American research university.

As we enter the last decade of the century, the country's universities, colleges, and community colleges together face an even greater challenge: To sustain the research infrastructure and also develop the climate, the support structures, the people, and the modified institutions necessary for meeting today's major national need, education of the highest quality for all students.

A few comments are in order concerning how we have gone about our work. The Committee on the Mathematical Sciences in the Year 2000 was asked to: (i) review the status of undergraduate mathematical sciences education in the United States; (ii) develop a plan for the revitalization of mathematics education at our nation's colleges and universities; and (iii) delineate responsibilities for the implementation of the plan. Appropriately, committee membership reflects a wide variety of perspectives and experience. Over the last three years we benefited from the extensive data gathering done by Bernard Madison in preparing our earlier publication, *A Challenge of Numbers*, and from the advice and opinions of thousands of mathematicians, scientists, and engineers. We are grateful to them for sharing their ideas through a variety of means: (i) two large national symposia we organized: *Calculus for a New Century* in late 1987 and *Mathematical Sciences: Servant to Other Disciplines* in 1989; (ii) two national meetings of department chairs, one organized by the Joint Policy Board for Mathematics and the other by the NRC's Board on Mathematical Sciences; (iii) discussions with the science policy committees of the American Mathematical Society (AMS) and the Mathematical Association of America (MAA) as well as the MAA Committee on the Undergraduate Program in Mathematics; (iv) dozens of presentation/discussion sessions at professional society meetings across the country including national meetings of AMS-MAA and the American Mathematical Association of Two Year Colleges (AMATYC); (v) two MS2000 workshops on human resources and curriculum; (vi) testimony presented at MS2000 Committee meetings; and (vii) hundreds of individual discussions conducted by committee members and staff interviews with selected department chairs and administrators.

Two circumstances have combined to enable *Moving Beyond Myths* to be a shorter report than might be expected from a three-year project. First, our Committee presented an overview of undergraduate mathematics education as part of *Everybody Counts — A Report to the Nation on the Future of Mathematics Education* (NRC 1989). Second, most of the supporting data for our work were presented in our 1990 report, *A Challenge of Numbers*. It might properly be viewed as an appendix to this final report, just as *Everybody Counts* might be considered its introduction.

We hope that the many groups to whom we have addressed our recommendations will move quickly to keep up the momentum of mathematics education change that has been building up over the last few years, and that a strong role will be played in the effort by our Committee's two NRC parent bodies: the Board on Mathematical Sciences and the Mathematical Sciences Education Board.

William E. Kirwan

William E. Kirwan
Chairman, MS2000 Committee
President
University of Maryland at College Park

CONTENTS

A Question of Size

Undergraduate mathematics is the second largest discipline taught at the post-secondary level. Each year 3.5 million students enroll in mathematics courses in the nation's vast and diverse system of higher education. One-third of these students take mathematics in two-year colleges and one-fourth in research universities, with the remainder—the greatest percentage—in comprehensive universities and liberal arts colleges. The total faculty numbers about 40,000, half of whom have a doctoral degree in the mathematical sciences. Mathematics accounts for approximately 10 percent of the total undergraduate course load in the United States and for approximately one-third of the science and engineering component of higher education.

*The national spotlight is turning on mathematics as
we appreciate its central role in the economic growth of
this country.*
                            —Calculus for a New Century, 1988

*History has taught us that the most important future
applications are likely to come from some unexpected
corner of mathematics.*
                            —Renewing U.S. Mathematics, 1990

THE CHALLENGE

Prosperity in today's global economy depends on scientific and technological strength, which in turn is built on the foundation of mathematics education. It is no wonder, therefore, that mathematics is in the spotlight. As the foundation of science and engineering, mathematics offers a key to our nation's future.

At the college and university level—the focus of this report—mathematics forms the core of the quantitative skills needed by our nation's scientific, technical, and managerial work force, including the nation's future mathematics teachers. Yet even this system—the linchpin of mathematics education in the nation—is beset by weaknesses that threaten the health of U.S. science and technology:

- Interest in majoring in mathematics is at an all-time low among entering freshmen.

- Too few students study advanced mathematics.

- Major segments of our population are significantly underrepresented in mathematically-based fields.

- Fewer than 10 percent of students who complete calculus are Blacks, Hispanics, or disabled.

- Retirements from college and university mathematical sciences faculties will soon exceed current U.S. doctoral degree production.

- Women receive only one in five doctorates in mathematics.

In a technologically driven economy, mathematically literate employees more readily achieve positions of influence, whereas those who remain innumerate are often denied the economic and social benefits of productive jobs and stable employment. Far from achieving its ideal as an agent for social equalization, undergraduate mathematics education as currently practiced bestows uneven benefits on different groups within our society—white males learn much more, women and many minorities much less. The result has been a growing polarization of society along the dimension of mathematical power that will, if left unchecked, exacerbate social and economic tensions by widening disparities in opportunities and earning capacities.

Most faculty who teach mathematics in colleges and universities are dedicated teachers. Many have written textbooks and helped lead curriculum development. Nevertheless, deficiencies in mathematics education are pervasive throughout the U.S. system of education. The size of undergraduate mathematics by itself creates tremendous inertia which impedes reform.

Some of the most entrenched problems are being successfully attacked through local action—one project and one campus at a time:

- Pilot projects to reform the way calculus and other introductory courses are taught and learned.

- Professional development initiatives that launch under-prepared students on successful college careers in science and mathematics.

- Talented youth programs that excite students for careers in mathematics and science.

- Programs for mathematics majors that address student needs and build personal self-confidence.

- Calculator methods and computer labs that transform traditional courses to meet the needs of a technological age.

- Networks, collaboratives, and workshops that enhance the professional competence of school teachers.

Initiatives such as these provide both grounds for optimism and models for more widespread improvement. Their successes help dispel common myths that impede reform. They demonstrate that we know how to do better. For those who have worked hard on educational issues, it is time for redoubled effort; for those who have not, it is time to begin.

Just as U.S. mathematics has achieved worldwide preeminence, so now we are called on to achieve the same stature in mathematics education. The nation's reward will be sustained health in science, industry, and the economy.

Profiles of Institutions of Higher Education

Community Colleges

People in America have a deep-seated belief that education is the path to a better life. Yet it seems that in our society that belief is not inculcated in the young, because a very large number drop out before high school graduation or stop out at graduation to work because of economic need. However, of those who drop out, stop out, or find themselves in life situations that are unsatisfactory, many will look later for opportunities for more education. A common statistic cited by community colleges is that the mean age of their student body is "thirty-something." The typical community college offers educational opportunity to adults, as well as educating those newly out of high school.

Any community college will contain students from all age levels and with many educational goals. An examination of the institution reveals a multi-purpose mission covering a broad spectrum of community needs. Although junior colleges were established to provide the first half of a bachelor's degree for the location-bound or economically less able student, very quickly they became the community college with a greatly expanded mission, including preparation for university transfer, post-secondary liberal arts education, technical courses and practical training for specific jobs, vocational degree programs, developmental instruction for those with weak academic skills, retraining programs for local businesses, multicultural education, English as a second language, continuing education activities, enrichment courses for senior citizens, literacy tutor training, and non-credit programs on community issues such as health, nutrition, insurance, finance, and law.

There are nearly 1400 two-year colleges in the United States with a total enrollment of nearly 5 million students, 25 percent of whom are enrolled in mathematics or statistics courses offered by approximately 1150 departments. Of these departments, 90 percent had mathematics or statistics programs and 70 percent offered some type of degree. The number of full-time faculty members in mathematics and statistics departments is 6600, with another 11,600 individuals teaching on a part-time basis. Almost 90 percent of the instruction by this faculty was below the calculus level, and 90 percent of the instruction is devoted to non-majors. Collectively, two-year colleges enroll nearly 40 percent of all undergraduate students and account for nearly 40 percent of all undergraduate mathematics course enrollments. Nearly 10 percent of U.S. students who receive a doctorate in the mathematical sciences began their undergraduate studies in a two-year college.

Liberal Arts Colleges

Approximately half of the bachelor's degree-granting institutions in the United States are small four-year colleges whose mission is to provide a broad, liberal education. Primarily residential, most of these colleges tend to serve regional constituencies, although a few well-known institutions have a more national character. Most liberal arts colleges have 1200-2000 students, virtually all of whom are between 18 and 22 years old. Largely because of their success in promoting a community of learners, these colleges are unusually productive as a source of Ph.D. scientists and mathematicians. Most of these institutions also prepare teachers through programs that involve their departments of mathematics and science in essential leadership roles.

In the majority of liberal arts colleges, 3-5 percent of the graduates major in mathematics—several times the national average. Faculty in these departments devote most of their energy to teaching and advising : they generally teach three or four courses each term, supervise several independent study projects, and advise students—especially first-year students—about their entire college program. In matters of appointment, reappointment, tenure, and promotions, liberal arts colleges emphasize teaching as a top priority together with scholarship in a broad context, including research, curriculum development, expository writing, and professional leadership.

Of the approximately 1000 four-year liberal arts colleges, more than 80 percent are private. The total enrollment is approximately 560,000 students, more than half of whom are enrolled in mathematics or statistics courses. There were 3450 full-time and 1550 part-time faculty members in mathematical sciences departments at four-year colleges, with 33 percent of the faculty teaching at least one course at the remedial level and 68 percent teaching courses at the pre-calculus level. Virtually all liberal arts colleges offer mathematical sciences programs, and more than 90 percent offer undergraduate majors in mathematics or statistics. Liberal arts colleges enroll approximately 10 percent of the nation's undergraduate students; their graduates account for one in six U.S. students who receive a Ph.D. in the mathematical sciences.

Comprehensive Universities

The comprehensive university, in structure and mission, is situated between the liberal arts college and the major research university. This segment of higher education is growing in size and now accounts for nearly 40 percent of the total enrollment in baccalaureate institutions.

Generally, comprehensive universities are relatively large, state-funded universities that offer degrees in all the traditional liberal arts and sciences and in most professional areas. Responsibility for professional programs is an important ingredient in the definition of a comprehensive university. Since in many cases comprehensive universities grew out of normal schools or the state colleges of education, undergraduate instruction is still their basic mission. Today, however, they offer numerous master's degrees, but few programs leading to the doctorate. Their faculties consist primarily of individuals holding Ph.D. degrees from major research universities. The student body is typically older, part-time, and diverse. Average test scores and other performance measures for students entering the comprehensive universities are usually lower than those of students entering land-grant, Ph.D.-granting institutions in the state.

Because of their historical ties to education and a primary mission of undergraduate teaching, the comprehensive university more commonly has small class sections in the introductory mathematics courses than does the research university. Since doctoral programs seldom exist, there are fewer graduate students available; hence introductory courses are taught by faculty. Although both faculty and administration seek to encourage scholarship and research, the resources for such activities are often not part of the institution's budgets and federal and private funding agencies are less likely to support mathematics or scientific research in institutions without Ph.D. programs. Nevertheless, despite heavy teaching responsibility and lack of funds, a portion of the faculty do successfully conduct quality basic research. The balance of commitment to scholarship and to teaching that resides in these highly trained faculties provides fertile soil for the seeds of change in undergraduate mathematics education.

Comprehensive universities enroll approximately 2.7 million undergraduates; total enrollment in mathematical sciences courses exceeds 650,000. Approximately 85 percent of the students in these institutions take at least one mathematics course during their studies. The approximately 400 comprehensive universities employ 6250 full-time and 3050 part-time faculty members in the mathematical sciences. About 4 percent of the mathematical sciences departments in these universities offer a doctorate, 38 percent offer a master's, and 56 percent a bachelor's as the highest degree. Graduates of comprehensive universities account for one in six U.S. students who receive a Ph.D. in the mathematical sciences.

Research Universities

A research university is a large, complex institution with a multiplicity of purposes. A large staff of researchers, postdoctoral fellows, and other professionals as well as faculty and students, both graduate and undergraduate are involved in research, education, and service. The nation, the states, and local communities rely on research universities for most of the basic research that is done in the United States as well as for a large part of the applied research. Research universities educate a large proportion of the scholars, researchers, and teachers not only for schools, colleges, and universities but also for business and industry. With few exceptions, all doctoral degrees awarded in the United States are from research universities.

This multiplicity of purposes and constituencies is reflected in the budget of a research university, which is typically several hundred million dollars and is drawn from many sources, including federal agencies, state and local governments, foundations, industry, and tuition. This broad base of support applies whether the institution is public or private.

Research and graduate education are often seen as the primary mission of a research university, especially in engineering and the sciences. This emphasis often influences other priorities, although concern for undergraduate teaching is a growing concern. States and the nation look increasingly to research universities for economic development and to maintain or regain economic competitiveness. Finally, society also looks to research universities for leadership in health care and social programs.

Faced with this overwhelming set of institutional responsibilities, a department of mathematical sciences at a research university is pulled in many directions. It is called on to teach mathematics (often including statistics) at all levels to an increasing number of students; to maintain research excellence and help support such excellence in engineering and the sciences; to help support the renewal and invigoration of school mathematics; and to help recruit and attract American students to mathematics and areas depending on mathematics.

Research universities enroll over 2.5 million undergraduates. Approximately 190 of the 260 research universities in the United States offer a doctoral program in mathematics or statistics. There are 735,000 students enrolled in mathematical sciences courses at these institutions and 6800 full-time faculty members. About two out of three students take at least one mathematics or statistics course; two-thirds of the total enrollment is generated by students not majoring in the mathematical sciences. Over 75 percent of instruction is at the calculus level or lower; only 4 percent is at the graduate level. Research universities collectively award 40 percent of the bachelor's degrees, 75 percent of the master's degrees, and nearly 100 percent of the doctoral degrees in mathematics. Baccalaureate graduates of research universities account for two out of every three U.S. students who receive a Ph.D. in the mathematical sciences.

Public acceptance of deficient standards contributes significantly to poor performance in mathematics education.

—Everybody Counts, 1989

THE MYTHS

Mathematics education cannot be effective without strong support from society. Unfortunately, misconceptions about mathematics are deeply rooted in school and society, in home and family. From students' early years colleges inherit an enormous deficit of scholarly maturity. Interest payments on this deficit balloon college enrollments in remedial and school-level mathematics courses. Indeed, about two-thirds of all college mathematics enrollments are in school-level courses (below the level of calculus). In America today, the profile of mathematics in higher education is not much different from that of mathematics in high school.

The source of many of these difficulties can be found in public (and parental) attitudes about mathematics that are rooted more in myth than in reality:

Building Confidence

At Spelman College in Atlanta, 8 percent of the graduates major in mathematics—a rate far greater than the national average of 1.6 percent.

The success of the mathematics and natural science program at Spelman is due to the special attention given to students that builds their confidence in their own ability to master mathematics. All natural science students participate in an eight-week summer program prior to the beginning of their first year, during which study skills are developed and role models are established. This careful mentoring is continued throughout the undergraduate program and develops into opportunities for research experiences and special honors sections. The faculty devotes a great deal of energy to advising, since student motivation is the most powerful factor in learning.

Not only does Spelman produce a large number of minority mathematicians and scientists, but its NASA Program for Women in Science and Engineering graduates a higher-than-average percentage of women mathematics majors who go on to pursue graduate studies in mathematics.

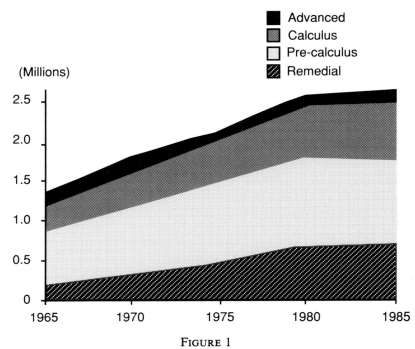

FIGURE 1
Total undergraduate enrollment in mathematical sciences departments at U.S. colleges and universities.

Myth: *Success in mathematics depends more on innate ability than on hard work.*

Reality: Sustained effort can carry most students to a satisfactory level of achievement in mathematics. Compare music and mathematics: although in both areas genetic factors clearly play a role at the very highest levels of creative achievement, parents and teachers generally believe that children can learn to play music at a reasonable level if only they exert sufficient effort. As a consequence, many students achieve success and personal satisfaction from their study of music. Whenever parents or teachers believe that genetic ability is the primary factor contributing to success in mathematics, students are likely to fail before they begin; when expectations of success are high, so is the resulting performance.

Myth: *Women and members of certain ethnic groups are less capable in mathematics.*

Reality: The popular notion that women, Blacks, and Hispanics "can't do math" is just an expression of ignorance or prejudice. Ample evidence shows such beliefs to be false. Experiences of countries such as Holland and Japan belie this myth, as do results from numerous innovative programs in the United States. Such examples demonstrate unequivocally that most college students can succeed in mathematics when learning takes place in an appropriate structure and context.

Myth: *Most jobs require little mathematics.*

Reality: The truth is just the opposite: more and more jobs—especially those involving the use of computers—require the capability to employ sophisticated quantitative skills. Although a working knowledge of arithmetic may have sufficed for jobs of the past, it is clearly not enough for today, for the next decade, or for the next century.

Myth: *All useful mathematics was discovered long ago.*

Reality: Mathematical discoveries are essential for industrial competitiveness. Without advances in mathematics we would have neither telephones nor computers, neither jet airplanes nor international banking. Technology depends on both old and new mathematics for innovation and power. Indeed, more new mathematics is being created and used each year than ever before in history.

Mathematics in Action

One way to link undergraduate mathematics to industrial research and development is through student projects in mathematical modelling. Many such programs are patterned after the Mathematics Clinic, which began at Harvey Mudd College nearly twenty years ago. In these programs, which now operate in dozens of institutions, a team consisting of one or more faculty and several students works on an unsolved mathematically oriented problem that comes from a company or government agency.

The problems are usually openended and must first be cut down to a manageable size. Faculty leaders assist with the mathematical model and give "short courses" on the mathematics that seems to be needed. Different students work on different parts of the problem, parts that suit their interests and expertise, but teamwork is the mode of operation. Students must make formal oral presentations in terms understandable to the client; as a result, they develop strong expository skills. Written reports are submitted to the client at the end of the project, and so the writing involved in these reports is also a part of the students' education.

Myth: *To do mathematics is to calculate answers.*

Reality: Rarely do workers or researchers confront mathematical problems requiring primarily calculation. Authentic problems are often ambiguous, admitting many forms and several answers. Mathematical power is revealed as much by the act of identifying and properly posing problems as by application of specific techniques and algorithms.

Myth: *Only scientists and engineers need to study mathematics.*

Reality: Mathematics is a science of patterns that is useful in many areas. Indeed, the most rapid areas of growth in applications of mathematics have been in the social, biological, and behavioral sciences. Financial analysts, legal scholars, political pollsters, and sales managers all rely on sophisticated mathematical models to analyze data and make projections. Even artists and musicians use mathematically based computer programs to aid in their work. No longer just a tool for the physical sciences, mathematics is a language for all disciplines.

If these myths were benign, with effects limited to the ignorance of those who believe them, they might be safely ignored. But ignorance in parents and teachers begets ignorance in students. Harmful myths about mathematics metastasize to the body politic, spreading ignorance and excusing underachievement throughout society. Efforts to eradicate these pernicious myths will require sustained support at all educational levels, but especially in colleges and universities where society's leaders are educated.

Undergraduate mathematics is the bridge between research and schools and holds the power of reform in mathematics education.

—Everybody Counts, 1989

No other collegiate discipline teaches as many students with such widely differing levels of preparation as does mathematics.

—A Challenge of Numbers, 1990

BEHIND THE MYTHS

Undergraduate mathematics plays a pivotal role in our system of mathematics education. It is in college where our nation's engineers and technicians are educated, where future scientists are recruited, and where many of society's leaders acquire basic quantitative skills. In addition, the instructional traditions of undergraduate mathematics form the model for all future teachers of mathematics.

Undergraduate mathematics is also a source of much of the mythology about mathematics that pervades society. Adults' attitudes about mathematics are largely shaped by their own experiences as students in school or college and by images created by media leaders. School teachers, politicians, writers, editors—all those whose careers influence the public's image of mathematics—view mathematics through a lens that was polished by their own education. Important clues to the widespread public misunderstanding of mathematics can be found in the traditions and habits of mathematics departments in colleges and universities across the nation.

Departments Under Stress

In the last twenty years the demand for undergraduate mathematics courses has risen more than twice as fast as have faculty resources in departments of mathematical sciences. Increased demand is due both to demographic and

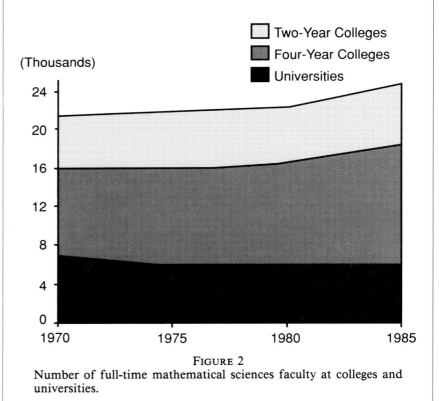

FIGURE 2

Number of full-time mathematical sciences faculty at colleges and universities.

social trends and to an increase in the use of mathematics in other disciplines. Consequently, today's students are much more diverse in mathematical preparation and needs. But since 1970, enrollments have increased by more than 70 percent while faculty size has increased by less than 30 percent. As a result, a faculty increase of more than 30 percent would be required today to recapture the student-faculty ratio of twenty years ago.

Rather than articulating forcefully the need to keep student-faculty ratios within reasonable bounds, the mathematics community sought to handle the increased workload in inexpensive ways, such as larger classes and increased use of graduate teaching assistants and part-time faculty. As a consequence, the image of mathematics as a low-cost, high-enrollment discipline became institutionalized on many campuses. It remains so today.

The last thirty years have also been a period of extraordinary achievements in mathematical research, during which time federal agencies and research universities elevated their research mission over their educational mission. Intensified competition for research funding created a climate in mathematics departments in which research accomplishments received increasing prestige, while contributions to improving education received lower priority. As a consequence, innovations in undergraduate teaching lag far behind advances in research. Both in instructional methodology and in curricular content, undergraduate mathematics is far below what it should be to best serve today's students. What is required is a balanced commitment to scholarship and instruction.

For a variety of reasons, not least being the ambivalent atmosphere in many college and university mathematics departments, interest in teaching college mathematics has declined significantly at both undergraduate and graduate levels. This trend is compounded by projections of impending retirements that foretell a severe future shortage in the number of college mathematics teachers. This situation has serious implications for the quality of mathematics education at all levels and for the related human resource needs of our nation.

Quantitative Reasoning

The demands of today's technological society require a work force that can understand complex processes, develop and test hypotheses, and draw logical conclusions. Innovative courses, set in the context of students' interests, have proven far more effective as a means of teaching this type of quantitative reasoning than have traditional requirements such as college algebra or elementary statistics.

One successful course of this type was developed at Mount Holyoke College as part of the New Liberal Arts initiative supported by the Sloan Foundation. A collection of case studies allows students to develop an appreciation of graphical techniques, approximation methods, and statistical concepts. Using a combination of lectures, laboratory sessions, and small discussion groups, the students work on three case studies:

- *Narrative and Numbers: Salem Village Witchcraft;*

- *Measuring and Modelling Difference: Aptitude and Achievement;*

- *Rates of Change: Population and Resources, Predation, and Disease.*

Computers are used as the primary tool in the analysis of these case studies, and for writing papers, manipulating data, and creating graphical images. Although not required, the course is now elected by more than one-third of the students at Mount Holyoke.

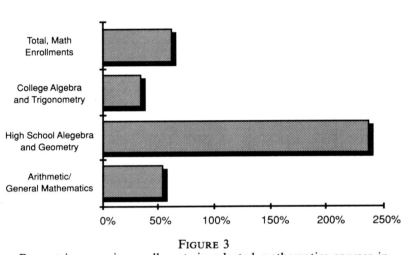

FIGURE 3

Percent increase in enrollments in selected mathematics courses in colleges and universities, 1965 to 1985.

For far too long, myth has substituted for reality in the U.S. approach to mathematics education. Mathematics departments find themselves trapped in institutional structures that assume that the instructional practices that have evolved over the past thirty years in mathematics are appropriate and acceptable. The result is a dysfunctional system of undergraduate mathematics beset on all sides by inadequacies and deficiencies:

- *In mathematical preparation of students:* Most U.S. students do not acquire quantitative skills sufficient for future study or careers. The evidence is all around us: chronically high attrition rates in mathematics courses at all levels, increasing numbers of college students enrolled in remedial courses, and international comparisons that show U.S.

students lagging far behind students from other countries. Although many students enter college having completed a year or more of calculus, a sizable proportion of undergraduates have difficulty even with elementary arithmetic. Many college students find themselves unready to begin standard college mathematics courses.

- *In support and reward for teaching:* Few universities offer much incentive for developing new approaches to teaching. Resources for instruction are meager and tend to reinforce reliance on large classes and packaged learning. The reward structure at most universities undervalues innovation in teaching or evidence of improved learning.

- *In teaching methods, course content, and instructional materials:* The way mathematics is taught at most colleges— by lectures—has changed little over the past 300 years, despite mounting evidence that the lecture-recitation method works well only for a relatively small proportion of students. Moreover, the syllabi of many undergraduate mathematics courses and the template-style textbooks are detached from the life experiences of students and are seen by many students as irrelevant.

- *In the use of computers in undergraduate mathematics:* Nothing in recent times has had as great an impact on mathematics as computers, yet in most college courses mathematics is still taught just as it was 30 years ago— as a cerebral, paper-and-pencil discipline for which computers either are irrelevant or can be ignored. Computers serve mathematics these days as indispensable aids in research and application. Yet only in isolated experimental courses has the impact of computing on the practice of mathematics penetrated the undergraduate curriculum.

- *In resources that support undergraduate mathematics:* The typical college or university mathematics department has been viewed historically as a source of large enrollments with low costs of instruction—a "cash cow" for institutional budgets. In contrast, departments of science and engineering have large budgets to support their established

"The losses of mathematical talent are not evenly distributed among racial and ethnic groups or the sexes. At each critical juncture in the pipeline more women and minority students drop out than do white males."
—A Challenge of Numbers, 1990

Mathematics for the Masses

At a large midwestern state university with over 50,000 students, the average enrollment in mathematics courses during the fall term is approximately 16,000. The mathematics department has about 125 full-time (FTE) faculty members, 225 graduate teaching assistants (more than half of whom are foreign nationals, and a quarter of whom come from other departments), and 25 undergraduate instructional aides. The circumstances of mathematics instruction in this institution are typical of many major research universities.

Service and lower-level courses dominate the teaching load with enrollments of over 14,000, ninety percent of the total. One such course, taken by approximately 1400 students, is taught by 45 teaching assistants and 6 part-time lecturers, all working under the supervision of one faculty member as a half-time assignment. Over 55 percent of the total faculty teaching effort in the department is devoted to the 11 percent of students enrolled in upper-division and graduate courses; only 22 percent of faculty effort is assigned to the 67 percent of students enrolled in precalculus mathematics courses.

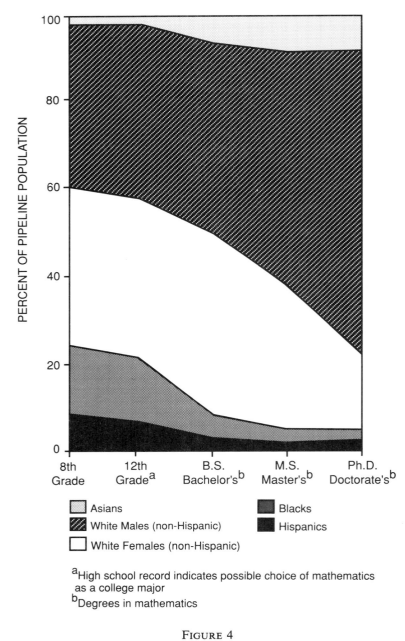

aHigh school record indicates possible choice of mathematics as a college major
bDegrees in mathematics

FIGURE 4
A representation of U.S. students in the mathematics pipeline.

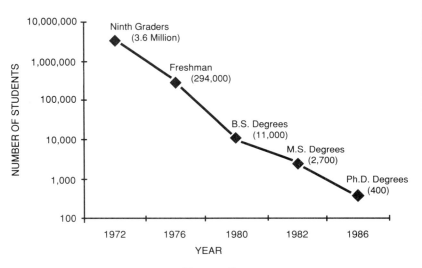

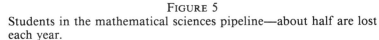

FIGURE 5

Students in the mathematical sciences pipeline—about half are lost each year.

needs for instructional and research laboratories. Even though the role of technology—hence of computer labs— in mathematics has grown in recent years, most mathematics departments still operate with budget allocations that, when compared with those for other departments, are among the smallest per credit hour of instruction. The resources available to most departments of mathematics are insufficient to meet their responsibilities.

- *In the number of minorities and women who study mathematics:* College mathematics attracts far too few Black and Hispanic students, and their attrition rates between high school and the sophomore year of college are much too high. Although the number of women enrolled in un-

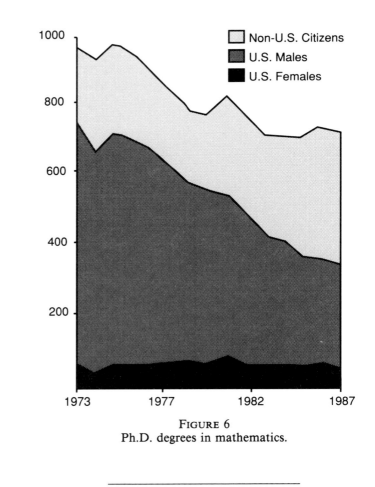

FIGURE 6
Ph.D. degrees in mathematics.

dergraduate mathematics courses is only slightly smaller than the number of men, the relative number of women drops dramatically in graduate enrollments. Only a small fraction of our population—consisting primarily of white males—complete a mathematics education that matches their potential and interests. The result is an appalling waste of human potential, denying to individuals opportunity for productive careers and to the nation the resources for economic strength.

- *In the number of students who study mathematics:* The number of students electing to take mathematics courses declines precipitously from ninth grade to graduate school. Each year from high school through graduate school, on average, one of every two students stops taking mathematics courses.

- *In the number of new engineers and scientists:* As students discontinue prematurely their study of mathematics, the quantitative skills of our work force fall behind the requirements of an international economy. Moreover, the number of individuals in their mid-twenties will decline until the end of this century, making it increasingly difficult to sustain present production of new engineers and scientists.

- *In the number of qualified school mathematics teachers:* Although many teachers hold certificates, few school teachers meet the standards for curriculum and professional preparation set forth by the National Council of Teachers of Mathematics. In addition, half the nation's mathematics teachers will leave teaching by the year 2000.

- *In the number of U.S. mathematics graduate students:* The number of U.S. students who pursue graduate studies in mathematics is now much smaller than it was twenty years ago. Today only one in every ten thousand students enrolled in ninth grade mathematics will pursue and eventually earn a doctorate in the mathematical sciences, far too few to replace retiring faculty in coming decades. Although shortfalls in U.S. mathematics students can be mitigated to some extent by immigration, current trends portend a serious future shortage of mathematical sciences faculty.

*What we urgently need today is a more inclusive
view of what it means to be a scholar—a recognition
that knowledge is acquired through research, through
synthesis, through practice, and through teaching.*
                    —Scholarship Reconsidered, 1990

FACING THE MYTHS

America's system of higher education is the envy of the
world. Institutional variety matches the variety of our population: two-year colleges, liberal arts colleges, women's colleges, historically Black colleges and universities, comprehensive universities, research universities—not to mention
a variety of specialized institutions. Diverse, robust, and
infinitely varied, U.S. higher education offers students from
around the world courses to suit every whim and programs
to meet every need. Nevertheless, the overall balance of
the system seems no longer to serve well the needs of U.S.
society. Industry, education, military, and government per-
sonnel offices all report difficulties in finding employees with
the skills required for productive work. The American pub-

An innovative calculus course at the University of Illinois uses the full symbolic, numeric, graphic, and text capabilities of a powerful computer algebra system. Significantly, there is no textbook for this course—only a sequence of electronic notebooks.

Each notebook begins with basic problems introducing new ideas, followed by tutorial problems on techniques and applications. Both problem sets have "electronically active" solutions to support student learning. The notebook closes with a section called "Give-it-a-try," where no solutions are given. Students use both the built-in word processor and the graphic and calculating software to build their own notebooks to solve these problems, which are submitted electronically for comments and grading.

Notebooks have the versatility to allow re-working of examples with different numbers and functions, to provide for the insertion of commentary to explain concepts, to incorporate graphs and plots as desired by students, and to launch routines that extend the complexity of the problem. The instructional focus is on the computer laboratory and the electronic notebook, with less than one hour per week spent in the classroom. Students spend more time than in a traditional course and arrive at a better understanding, since they have freedom to investigate, rethink, redo, and adapt. Moreover, creating course notebooks strengthens students' sense of accomplishment.

lic is now demanding accountability—both from schools and from higher education.

America's record in mathematical research is, likewise, the envy of the mathematical world. This preeminence is documented not only in objective measures (e.g., research productivity, international awards) but also in the steady stream of international students and researchers who visit our premier universities. The challenge we now face is to elevate U.S. mathematics education to the same high level of achievement and reputation as U.S. mathematical research.

To attack this problem successfully, mathematicians and university administrators need first to examine carefully the circumstances that give rise to inadequacies and deficiencies. Surely the twin burdens of increased enrollments and erosion of support have left many departments without the resources needed to fulfill their educational and intellectual responsibilities. But there is more to the problem than inadequate resources. A plan to revitalize mathematics education must be built on a careful analysis of current deficiencies.

Wasted Breath

Since virtually all mathematics teachers received the majority of their mathematics instruction in traditional lecture courses, it is not surprising that lecturing has continued to be the most common way that mathematics is taught, both in high school and in college. To believe that one can teach mathematics successfully by lectures, one must believe what most mathematicians know to be untrue—that mathematics can be learned by watching someone else do it correctly. Research shows clearly that this method of teaching does little to help beginning students learn mathematics, a fact underscored by the staggering rates of withdrawal or failure among students who take introductory college mathematics courses.

It is widely recognized that lectures place students in a passive role, failing to engage them in their own learning. Even students who survive such courses often absorb a very misleading impression of mathematics—as a collection of skills with no connection to critical reasoning. Yet despite its recognized ineffectiveness for most mathematics students, lecturing continues as the dominant form of instruction in mathematics classrooms because it is inexpensive: neither faculty members nor administrators have to invest heavily in mathematics courses taught in the traditional lecture style.

Perhaps even more mysterious is the virtual absence of computers from undergraduate mathematics. Computers have changed significantly the practice of mathematics at all levels, from routine application to advanced research. Computers also enhance student motivation, provide natural catalysts for teamwork, and focus faculty attention on the process of learning. Unless undergraduate mathematics courses are revised to reflect the impact of computers on the practice of mathematics, students will continue to perceive mathematics as a discipline disconnected from reality.

Missing Context

The unease with which many students regard mathematics begins early in their education and is all too regularly reinforced through their school years. The situation seldom improves, not even in college. Students often find themselves in classes in which little effort is made to place the subject matter in a context that is meaningful to the student. Mathematics becomes not a powerful tool but an overwhelming barrier that students must surmount to enter their chosen disciplines. For such students, undoubtedly the majority, mathematics continues to be a mystery unrelated to other subjects or problems in the real world.

Absent a conscious effort to set mathematics in the context of learners' experiences, mastery of skills (including vocabulary, notation, and procedures) serves no legitimate educational purpose. Students who endure such instruction come to regard mathematics as a ritual irrelevant to their own lives. Upon becoming parents, such students impart the same attitude about mathematics to their children.

It is virtually impossible to cover well in a single course both the many ways in which mathematics is applied and the range of topics needed to support authentic applications. As

NSF Calculus Initiative

As the pivotal course in the scientific curriculum, calculus has long been a natural focus for debate when discussions turn to educational reform. In the mid-1980s, talk turned to action when the National Science Foundation launched a major initiative to foster improvement in the quality of calculus instruction on a national scale.

Begun in 1988, the program made over 50 awards totaling nearly $7 million during its first three years of operation. The results of the individual calculus projects are still to be evaluated, but one great benefit is already evident—the enthusiasm generated in hundreds of mathematical sciences departments for improvement in the teaching of calculus.

NSF expects to expand the scope of this initiative to eventually encompass the entire undergraduate curriculum.

"The real impact of technology is the opportunity it provides for students to explore, to work in groups, to write laboratory reports, and undertake projects."

—*Priming the Calculus Pump, 1990*

25

Priming the Pump

In response to the growing concern in recent years about undergraduate mathematics, many projects have emerged to explore new approaches to instruction or to study particular issues in depth. Examples:

- *Preparing Teachers. A guide for mathematics departments to curricula that will educate intending teachers in a way to meet contemporary standards is contained in the 1991 MAA report A Call for Change: Recommendations for the Mathematical Preparation of Teachers of Mathematics and the 1991 NCTM document Professional Standards for Teaching Mathematics.*

- *Undergraduate Research. Reports on a wide variety of effective programs that provide research experiences to undergraduate students of mathematics appear in the 1990 MAA volume Models for Undergraduate Research in Mathematics.*

- *Calculus Reform. Nearly one hundred projects, the tip of the iceberg, are presented in the 1990 MAA publication Priming the Calculus Pump: Innovations and Resources.*

- *Doctoral Study. The Board on Mathematical Sciences is conducting a study to identify features of successful doctoral and postdoctoral programs which contribute to the preparation of productive members of the mathematical community.*

continued on next page

a result, many introductory college courses offer students—frequently with disastrous results—a distilled mathematical essence that is, from a student's perspective, devoid of meaning. Particularly at beginning levels, where students from various disciplines take the same courses, this common approach isolates mathematics from the very subjects for which mathematics students are preparing themselves.

Upper-division courses often exhibit a similar profile, albeit for different reasons. Many advanced mathematics courses are taught primarily in a style that will prepare students for graduate study in mathematics. Consequently, they address insufficiently the needs of the majority of students who intend either to enter the job market with a bachelor's degree or to pursue graduate work in another discipline. From beginning to end, undergraduate mathematics has been relatively unresponsive to the changing role of mathematics in society and to the changing needs of students in our colleges.

Casual Teaching

In many university mathematics departments, mathematical stature is defined by research. Faculty play an effective role in mentoring graduate students from their role as student to the position of junior colleague. But undergraduate teaching, especially elementary teaching, can under these circumstances be too easily viewed as an ancillary responsibility. Because professional attitudes are shaped primarily while students are in graduate school, the culture of the leading research departments has a subtle but nonetheless very real influence even in the majority of institutions where teaching is unquestionably the primary institutional objective. Although some institutions have taken steps to increase the priority of undergraduate teaching, the overall effect of graduate education is to perpetuate a system of rewards that undervalues teaching.

Faculty attitudes towards teaching are both reflected and perpetuated by the role assigned to graduate teaching assistants. At most universities that have graduate programs, teaching assistants staff the majority of lower-division courses, often assuming virtually complete responsibility for instruction and evaluation. Indeed, the practice of using teaching assistants is a structural feature of graduate support so ingrained that without it most departments could not survive on their present budgets. Heavy reliance on the use of graduate teaching assistants, many of whom have limited experience or training for the responsibilities placed on them, has far-reaching consequences.

Approximately half of the graduate mathematics students in the United States are nonresident foreigners. These students both need and merit support for their graduate studies: they contribute much to the strength and sophistication of graduate programs, and many will contribute significantly to mathematics and to society after they finish their degrees.

Few graduate students, however, are ready to serve well the educational needs of first-year college students; teaching in a foreign culture is particularly difficult for those who were not themselves educated in U.S. schools. Experience in teaching, mathematical expectations, communication skills, cross-cultural sensitivity, and familiarity with technology are vitally important issues that frequently take considerable time to develop—especially among those who are new to this country. The special need for sensitivity toward all students that is required to attract more women and underrepresented minorities into mathematics underscores the important role that graduate teaching assistants play in nurturing students in the mathematical sciences.

Few universities recognize explicitly in the design of their graduate mathematics programs that the future careers of most of their doctoral students will be devoted primarily to undergraduate teaching. Few if any mathematics graduate programs attempt to familiarize graduate students with important curricular and policy issues of undergraduate education. Few graduate assistants undergo systematic training to prepare them for their lifelong role as teachers.

Our system of graduate education produces a cadre of college and university teachers who have little concept of teaching as a profession. Not only are mathematics graduate students denied significant opportunities to develop this

continued from previous page

- *Study in Depth. Advice for effective approaches to undergraduate majors is the focus of Challenges for College Mathematics: An Agenda for the Next Decade, a report prepared by a joint task force of the MAA and the Association of American Colleges as part of a multidiscipline study of undergraduate majors.*

"Beginning graduate students in the laboratory sciences may learn as much from advanced graduate students and postdoctorals as they do from the principal investigator—the group provides a mutually supportive and nurturing learning environment for all. The challenge for the mathematical sciences is to create an analogous environment for their own graduate students and postdoctorals."

—Renewing U.S. Mathematics, 1990

Linking with Schools

Many colleges and universities are developing outreach programs to help increase the professional competence of teachers of mathematics. Two examples:

- *The Special Projects Office in the School of Mathematics at the University of Minnesota coordinates a variety of outreach projects that bring together business leaders, government officials, and educators from the elementary school level through the university level to discuss policy issues and to advocate change. The activities include direct service projects such as the University of Minnesota Talented Youth Mathematics Program (UMTYMP) and an NSF Teacher Renewal Project, as well as networking projects such as the Minnesota Mathematics Mobilization, the Twin Cities Urban Mathematics Collaborative, and the Mathematicians and Education Reform network. Each of these activities builds on the expertise of college and university mathematicians.*

- *The Bay Area Mathematics Project, now in its eighth year, brings school mathematics teachers to Berkeley for a four-week summer program designed to improve their effectiveness as teachers. To increase the scope of the program, participants serve as teachers of other teachers and administrators when they return to their schools. The program has grown each year with funding provided by local community and civic organizations. Teachers from different grade levels are selected as participants so*

continued on next page

aspect of professional competence, but their graduate training frequently conveys the subtle message that undergraduate teaching is a second-class activity rather than a critical aspect of the profession.

Flawed Models

From grade school to graduate school, mathematics education revolves around the hub of undergraduate mathematics. Unfortunately, few university mathematics departments maintain meaningful links with mathematics in school or with the mathematical preparation of school teachers. Although one in four mathematics majors eventually teaches in school, instructional methods that are widely used in undergraduate programs foster a model of teaching—blackboard lectures, template exercises, isolated study, narrow tests—that is inappropriate for elementary and secondary school teachers. Similarly, most graduate doctoral programs place scant emphasis on preparing students to be effective at what most of them will do for their entire career—undergraduate teaching. All too often, new teachers embark on their careers with serious deficits of preparation in broad areas such as curriculum development, problem solving, and connections between mathematics and other disciplines.

Despite widespread efforts to establish effective standards for curriculum and instruction in school mathematics, undergraduate mathematics programs frequently perpetuate modes of delivery that are ineffective for most students and choices of content that are inappropriate for most prospective teachers. Only when college faculty begin to recognize by deed as well as word that preparing school teachers is of vital national importance can we expect to see significant improvement in the continuity of learning between school and college.

Few college mathematicians pay as much attention to advances in the study of teaching and learning as to advances in mathematical research. It is rare to find mathematics courses taken by prospective teachers that pay equal attention to strong mathematical content, innovative curricular materials, and awareness of what research reveals about how children learn mathematics. Unless college and university mathematicians model through their own teaching effective strategies that engage students in their own learning, school teachers will continue to present mathematics as a dry subject to be learned by imitation and memorization.

A similar concern must be expressed regarding the experiences of the graduate students who will become the next generation of college teachers. Only infrequently—more by accident than by plan—does the education of our future college teachers provide models of appropriate instructional techniques as well as intellectually challenging opportunities to address issues of how mathematics is taught and learned.

Outmoded Values

Because research institutions tend to establish values for the discipline, any reform of undergraduate mathematics education must address the question of how those values can be reshaped. Although attitudes are gradually changing on some campuses, it is still the case that at many institutions, teaching and research are viewed as competitive activities. In those universities whose basic charge is research and the granting of advanced degrees, academic survival depends on published research; in such institutions, undergraduate teaching offers few rewards. In contrast, at many colleges teaching loads are heavy and time for professional life is limited. The result is a schism in the profession that sunders the mathematical community into separate but decidedly unequal sectors.

Due to constraints on resources in many institutions, there is little mobility for faculty. Funding for research, which could support visits to other institutions, is very scarce. Financial support for activities that would contribute to the improvement of teaching is even more difficult to obtain. Thus many mathematics faculty members—especially those at smaller institutions—are professionally isolated, unable to keep abreast of modern developments in either teaching or research.

continued from previous page

that they can appreciate how their students are taught before and after they teach them. These teachers participate in hands-on problem sessions to learn how students learn, and they practice giving presentations that they can use to instruct their fellow teachers at their home schools. The success of the Bay Area Mathematics Project led to the American Mathematics Project, a collection of over 20 similar projects throughout the country jointly sponsored by the MAA and NCTM.

"One-third of the first and second year college students in the United States are enrolled in two-year colleges, including over two-thirds of Afro-American, Hispanic, and Native American students. It is clear from these figures that any effort to strengthen the undergraduate mathematics major, especially to recruit more majors among minority students, must be carried out in a manner that includes two-year colleges as a full partner...."

—*Challenges for College Mathematics: An Agenda for the Next Decade*

Effective Cooperation

At Austin Community College in Texas, nearly nine out of every ten students who transfer to public colleges and universities are still enrolled one year later. This measure of "one year survivability" of transfer students is nearly 40 percent higher than the state-wide average. Transfer success comes from paying attention to curriculum.

Almost every course at the college has been structured so that it will transfer directly to the two large neighboring state universities. The operative philosophy is that students should never find comparable courses at the community college easier because content is reduced or standards diluted. Classes should be easier only because they are smaller in size, because the faculty is more accessible and effective, or because the atmosphere is more supportive. The faculty is firm in its standards but caring in its approach to students.

College faculty have frequent contact with faculty at nearby universities, sometimes even influencing the university curriculum structure or choice of text. For example, a special program in mathematics, in place for over a decade, brings Austin Community College onto the University of Texas campus two nights a week to teach college algebra to university students. For these students, the university counts hours of enrollment at Austin Community College toward a student's minimum full-time enrollment obligation at the university.

Invisible Instructors

The great majority of mathematics faculty in U.S. colleges view themselves primarily as teachers, not as researchers. Moreover, most of these teachers' time and energy is devoted to developing the mathematical power of students who never will use higher mathematics. What their students need is quantitative literacy sufficient for life—for trades and vocations, for public affairs and private lives. The mathematical education of the great majority of students in American higher education is confined to introductory courses taught most often in two-year colleges or in the margins of university departments of mathematics.

The infrastructure of U.S. business depends on the fruits of these instructors' efforts. Their students will become the technicians and practitioners that support American manufacturing and transportation, farming and commerce. More often than not, minority students get their first chance at higher education in a two-year college, or in a small regional college; many such students are first-generation college students. Their access to advanced degrees depends on the momentum provided by this initial experience with higher education.

Yet in the world of higher education, instructors who undertake these tasks are virtually invisible. With rare exceptions, no graduate programs in mathematics focus on the task of preparing individuals for careers of teaching introductory, vocational, and technical mathematics. Few natural career paths exist for those who teach in two-year colleges, nor is there any visible reward system for those who devote their lives to this most fundamental work. In reality, the "mathematical community" is not really a community at all, since many of those who do the most important instructional work feel like outsiders in their own world.

Effective programs teach students, not just mathematics.
—Challenges for College Mathematics, 1990

MOVING BEYOND MYTHS

Responses to the problems facing undergraduate mathematics must occur on many fronts, including faculty members and their departments, colleges and universities, business and industry, professional societies, and government agencies. All those with a stake in mathematics must reassert the vital importance of effective undergraduate education in the mathematical sciences. Over the next decade, the mathematical community must restructure fundamentally the culture, content, and context of undergraduate mathematics education.

No one should underestimate the inertia that must be overcome in order to change the culture that controls undergraduate mathematics. Many agencies and constituencies

Producing Mathematics Majors

Clarence Stephens created at SUNY Potsdam an undergraduate mathematics program that is difficult to overlook. For nearly two decades mathematics has dominated this regional public college of 4000 students, both in terms of quality and quantity of students. In 1985 the college graduated 184 mathematics majors, a total exceeded only by two campuses of the University of California. Approximately 24 percent of the bachelor's degrees at SUNY Potsdam are in mathematics and over 40 percent of the college's honor students are mathematics majors.

Mathematics at SUNY Potsdam does not rely on novel use of technology or innovative curricula to attract students. "We focus on the human factor," Stephens says, "to change students' perception that mathematics is an almost impossible subject for students to learn and that only the most gifted can be expected to achieve any degree of success." The atmosphere makes mathematics students feel good about themselves; as a result of a supportive environment, they want to learn.

continued on next page

must join the campaign, including business and industry, government at all levels (federal, state, local), scientists and engineers, college and university administrators, and public officials. Broad support is necessary if significant improvement is to be possible. But it will require leadership to marshal that support in consistent and constructive directions. Leadership for reform is the responsibility of the faculty—of mathematicians in every institution of higher education, from comprehensive universities to two-year colleges, from liberal arts colleges to research universities.

In particular, mathematical sciences faculty must assume full responsibility for the mathematics education of *all* students. They must change the way mathematics is taught; increase substantially the participation of women, minorities, and the disabled; and play a more substantial role in the preparation of mathematics teachers. In a world in which productivity depends so heavily on quantitative literacy, everybody does count.

GOALS

- **Effective undergraduate mathematics instruction for all students.**

- **Full utilization of the mathematical potential of women, minorities, and the disabled.**

- **Active engagement of college and university mathematicians with school mathematics, especially in the preparation of teachers.**

- **A culture for mathematicians that respects and rewards teaching, research, and scholarship.**

continued from previous page

Over half of the freshman class takes calculus as an elective, and post-calculus courses account for 50 percent of total mathematics enrollments. The program recognizes every student's accomplishments and stresses the development of successful role models; faculty present just enough in courses for students to learn essential ideas, not so much as to overwhelm them. Tests are viewed as milestones in learning, not as measures for setting high or low levels of achievement. The program depends on a faculty dedicated to teaching and committed to students. The rewards for faculty are students who learn.

33

Achievement in mathematics is promoted by offering students an environment that fosters success. The Professional Development Program (PDP) at the University of California at Berkeley was developed ten years ago by Uri Treisman to redress excessive failure rates in calculus of Blacks with strong academic records. The program was developed in response to evidence that social isolation of minority students impeded their learning of calculus. It substituted for remedial efforts an approach to learning based on faculty involvement, academic challenge, collaborative learning, and growth of a student community. This approach to learning, which has always been a central part of the educational philosophy of the Historically Black Colleges and the private liberal arts colleges, has now been replicated in special programs in more than fifty universities.

One example is the Professional Development Program at California State Polytechnic University at Pomona. Another is the Emerging Scholars Program (ESP) at the University of Texas, Austin. In both cases the format is similar to that at Berkeley, with special recitation sections that meet for several two-hour sessions each week. Study groups integrate aspects of students' social and academic lives and encourage independent study habits. Key ingredients include high expectations of competence, strong academic components, capable instruction, cooperative learning, and commitment from students.

AN ACTION PLAN

Develop and Promulgate Effective Instructional Models:

Faculty:

Learn about learning • Think as deeply about how to teach as about what to teach • Query unexamined assumptions about education • Explore effective alternatives to "lecture and listen " • Involve students actively in the learning process • Emphasize practices known to be effective with minority students • Teach future teachers in the ways they will be expected to teach • Exploit modern technology fully • Teach the students you have, not the ones you wish you had.

Departments:

Develop effective programs targeting underrepresented groups • Adapt tested and proven models • Build a team of faculty to carry out experiments, and expose all faculty to the results • Start a departmental seminar on issues of teaching and learning • Assign the best teachers to introductory courses • Employ varied instructional approaches: group methods, writing, investigative assignments, laboratory projects • Recognize and support the extensive special effort required to introduce computers effectively into the curriculum • Use knowledge gleaned from minority projects • Sensitize teaching assistants to cultural impacts in the classroom • Vigorously recruit women, minorities, and disabled students to pursue careers in mathematics and science.

34

Colleges and Universities:

Form an institutional task force in response to *Moving Beyond Myths* • Work with other institutions of higher education to frame an initial state response • Use both responses to stimulate mathematical sciences departmental efforts • Provide resources for appropriate experimentation • Stimulate use of computers in mathematics teaching • Insist that departments mainstream rather than remediate students • Emphasize effectiveness in teaching • Begin an institutional effort to learn how to evaluate teaching properly • Recognize and reward educational innovation.

Professional Societies:

Investigate and publicize successful instructional models, especially for underrepresented groups • Launch nationwide programs to promulgate effective instructional models • Intensify efforts to inform faculty of the nature, magnitude, and urgency of the problems in undergraduate mathematics • Send peer consulting teams into departments • Establish a journal of undergraduate educational research and practice • Expand programs to educate the public on harmful effects of popular myths about mathematics • Develop and disseminate information on careers in mathematics-based fields • Encourage dialogue among school, college, and university faculty through joint meetings • Stimulate local, state, and national networks • Establish national mathematics education awards that recognize contributions in innovative curricular design, effective methods of teaching, and understanding of how mathematics is learned.

Government:

Give undergraduate mathematics high priority in education funding • Focus first on introductory subjects as a key to opportunity for disadvantaged groups • Support results-oriented experimentation • Invest in dissemination and pro-

Undergraduate Research

Undergraduate research, in which students experience for themselves the open-ended exploratory nature of mathematical investigation, is one of the proven means of launching students on successful careers in the mathematical sciences. However, during the ten-year hiatus in NSF support of undergraduate research, few institutions managed to sustain these programs on their own.

One exception is the University of Minnesota at Duluth, where Joe Gallian has, since 1977, directed a summer research program for undergraduates in mathematics. Faculty and students are imbedded in an informal, nurturing environment that is conducive to research and provides for necessary special attention. Each student is given a problem that has been carefully selected to meet the student's background and to sustain the student's interest. A publishable result is the stated goal for each experience.

Discussion and interaction are encouraged through weekly meetings in which partial results are presented, and by having the participants share living quarters so that they can communicate and work at home. Outings and weekly luncheons bring students and faculty advisors together on a social basis, but the discussions normally turn to mathematics. Preparation of manuscripts for publication often takes a year or more following the summer session, but in many cases these papers do appear in a mathematical or scientific journal.

Making Mathematics Work

During the last decade, as mathematics majors climbed nationally from 1 to 2 percent of baccalaureate degrees, mathematics majors at St. Olaf College in Northfield, Minnesota, rose from 8 to 16 percent of the college's graduates. In the last decade, over 30 graduates have earned doctorates in the mathematical sciences—averaging three per year from each graduating class.

St. Olaf is a liberal arts institution of 3000 students. Mathematics is promoted and taught as an excellent liberal arts major—a subject that opens doors to many disciplines. As a consequence, each year from first year through senior year, the number of intending mathematics majors increases. Faculty enthusiasm for mathematics is conveyed both in the classroom and through various social activities designed to promote an image on campus that it is fun to major in mathematics.

Faculty standards are made clear in a written departmental statement of professional expectations given to every prospective faculty member: teaching is top priority, supported by an active but broad professional record of scholarship or research. Teaching is formally evaluated both by peers and students and contributes significantly to reappointment decisions. Professional activity is defined in broad terms and is supported through a strong sabbatical program and other college funds for professional development.

continued on next page

mulgation of successful models • Broaden experimentation to encompass the full curriculum • Provide resources to support effective instructional methods • Augment graduate fellowship programs with a program of cash awards to undergraduate departments that produce the students • Expand support for programs that retain women and minorities in the mathematics pipeline, keying on critical transition points • Support efforts that ally groups in support of planned, systemic change.

Establish and Disseminate National Guidelines or Standards:

Professional Societies:

Develop and disseminate new advisory national guidelines for undergraduate and graduate programs dealing with curriculum, teaching, and evaluation • Align these with national standards for school mathematics • Focus on critical transitions: lower division to upper division, two-year college to university, undergraduate to graduate • Set specific targets for achieving parity for underrepresented groups • Relate guidelines to college and university accreditation • Conduct an in-depth study of resources for departments • Launch a visionary curriculum project aimed at the early decades of the next century.

Faculty:

Participate actively in professional societies' discussion and development of national goals and guidelines • Support and implement emerging guidelines for undergraduate and graduate mathematics • Become familiar with evidence that all students can learn mathematics • Teach as if each student is a national asset • Reinterpret "high standards" to mean that many students learn rather than that most students don't • Recognize that meeting such standards may require dramatic change in classroom practice • Approach teaching as a profession, not as a task • Set a stringent personal standard—that if my students don't learn, it is I (not my students or their previous teachers) who have failed.

continued from previous page

Mathematics faculty are professionally very active, both in research and in education. In the last twelve years, members of the Mathematics Department have received nearly $2 million in grants for projects related to undergraduate curriculum development, school outreach, faculty professional activity, and computer labs. One recent grant from the Fund for the Improvement of Post-Secondary Education (FIPSE) supports an innovative "teaching post-doc" program that provides new Ph.D.s with a two-year mentored transition to undergraduate teaching that provides time for research and for seminars on teaching and learning.

37

To provide national leadership in addressing problems that result in the under-representation of minorities in mathematics, the Mathematical Association of America has established project SUMMA—Strengthening Underrepresented Minority Mathematics Achievement. SUMMA is designed to stimulate fundamental changes in attitude and practice of the collegiate mathematics community in regard to the education of minority students. The project is organized around five key components:

- *Intervention projects for middle and secondary school students, using the MAA sections to develop and replicate effective intervention programs.*

- *Mainstreaming projects for college and university students, working in collaboration with the Dana Center at the University of California, Berkeley to assist mathematics departments in setting goals for minority participation and establishing programs that will achieve these goals.*

- *School and college mentorship programs, providing opportunities for minority professionals in the mathematical sciences to serve as mentors in communities, schools, and on campuses.*

- *Development assistance programs, informing mathematicians and minority students about funding opportunities for minority projects and providing technical assistance for the development of proposals.*

continued on next page

38

Departments:

Develop a five-year plan to transform departmental instruction based on national guidelines • Emphasize mathematics for all • Be results-oriented: increase success rates • Incorporate insights gained from departmental experimentation • Include specific plans for using computers, improving numeracy, teaching teachers, and supporting majors • Use national targets from professional societies for success of women and minorities • Set department targets to reduce dependence on teaching assistants and part-time instructors • Address the need to enlarge the scope of graduate programs in the mathematical sciences to include issues of curriculum, teaching, and learning • Relate the departmental plan to the weak state of research funding and to changes in school mathematics programs • Enlist the aid of professional societies in developing and implementing the departmental plan • Take the departmental plan to the administration • Offer higher success rates in exchange for resources needed to implement the plan.

Colleges and Universities:

Give top institutional priority to effective teaching • Judge teaching by results, not by process • Adopt a broad standard of professional responsibility encompassing teaching and scholarship as well as research • Utilize this broad standard in decisions about hiring, retention, salary, promotion, and tenure • Align institutional admissions and placement practices with contemporary standards for school mathematics • Set high institutional expectations for the mathematics performance of all students • Help develop a five-year state plan for undergraduate mathematics • Involve state mathematics coalitions to ensure close coupling to national and state goals for school mathematics • Help the mathematics department implement their five-year plan, injecting resources in planned stages as results become apparent.

Government:

Support the development of advisory national standards or guidelines • As consensus emerges, encourage undergraduate mathematics plans, proposals, and projects based on these guidelines • Develop governmental responses to revitalization of undergraduate mathematics • Coordinate across agencies • Recognize the key role played by professional societies, since changing values must be internalized over time by the mathematics community.

continued from previous page

• *Programs to attract minorities into teaching, disseminating information to students, teachers, and advisors at the high school and college levels, and encouraging the expansion of scholarship programs for promising minority students interested in teaching.*

Curricular Innovation

For the past several years the Exxon Foundation has helped Cornell University develop a series of innovative general education courses in mathematics. For example, a mathematician and an artist team-teach a course entitled "Mathematics and Art" that deals with the influence of mathematical ideas on art through concepts such as proportion, perspective, and projective geometry. Another course introduces students to the intellectual history of calculus by helping them read parts of the original classic mathematical treatises of the Greek philosophers, of Newton, and of Gauss, among others.

A third course, "From Space to Geometry," explores the ways in which geometry has been used throughout the centuries to try to explain the universe in which we live. Two other courses integrate the use of personal computers in novel ways. One of these developed a new collection of computer software to enable students to interactively understand important mathematical concepts at their own pace and from their own perspective.

Minority Access to Research Careers

Since 1975 the National Institutes of Health (NIH) have been administering a program dedicated to increasing the number of scientists in biomedical research who are members of minority groups. The program, Minority Access to Research Careers (MARC), supports biomedical research training for students and faculty members at colleges and universities with substantial minority enrollments. It operates through four programs:

- *Honors Undergraduate Research Training Grants: Designed to assist minority institutions in developing strong undergraduate science curricula, this program makes awards directly to minority institutions to support science courses and individual students. The student awards cover tuition and fees and carry a stipend of $8,500 per year; awardees are required to participate in two off-campus summer research experiences that often lead to publication of a scientific paper. Because of the recognition received through these research activities, many students are recruited for graduate study and are awarded support. In 1989 the program supported the equivalent of 410 full-time undergraduate students.*

- *Honors Predoctoral Fellowships: This program is designed to provide a further incentive to graduates of the Honors Undergraduate Program to obtain research training. Fellowships carrying tuition,*

continued on next page

*Build and Sustain
Supportive Attitudes and Structures:*

The President and Governors:

Expand efforts to inform the public of the importance of mathematics (and science) education • Retain the national education goal of being "first in the world " • Emphasize that revitalization of undergraduate education is essential for reaching this goal • Highlight mathematics education as a key to opportunity in our time • Designate someone on the senior scientific and educational staff as responsible for implementing this Action Plan.

Congress, State Legislators, Regents:

Insist that plans for reforming mathematics (and science) education encompass the undergraduate level • Put resources behind undergraduate revitalization • Support planned, systemic change, not isolated projects and programs.

Federal and State Agencies:

Create a network of regional centers for excellence in the teaching of mathematics • Support time spent at regional centers by teachers at all educational levels • Initiate major programs of postdoctoral teaching fellowships to enable beginning faculty to develop expertise in curriculum, teaching, and learning • Institute fellowship programs to enable faculty members to enhance teaching effectiveness through time spent at innovative centers and institutions • Increase significantly the numbers of predoctoral fellowships and research assistantships in mathematics • Work to reduce dependency on teaching assistants for undergraduate mathematics instruction • Support effective programs of financial incentives for students planning on teaching careers, emphasizing especially minority teachers • Significantly increase support for dissemination and public information activities • Provide sustained financial support for working alliances and networks to implement parts of this Action Plan.

Universities and Colleges:

Fully fund the cost of effective undergraduate mathematics teaching • Provide sufficient computer labs to enable mathematics courses to be taught with full computer support • Speak out about the importance of research funding for healthy undergraduate education • Support the concepts of predoctoral, postdoctoral, and mid-career fellowships for college and university teachers of mathematics.

Faculty and Departments:

Build faculty networks within institutions, linking user departments • Connect to networks of mathematicians committed to educational reform • Develop a strong presence in regional and national meetings of department chairs • Forge professional alliances and initiate collaborative projects with mathematics teachers in local schools • Offer regular enrichment programs that motivate school-age youth, especially minorities, to continue studying mathematics • Speak to needs and accomplishments in a second five-year plan for undergraduate mathematics.

Professional Societies and National Organizations:

Involve the broad constituencies of mathematics education in discussions of goals and standards • Sustain structures built to promulgate targeted minority programs • Support national transformation based on new guidelines • Establish structures linking corporations, minority action groups, and scientific societies to long-term revitalization effort.

continued from previous page

fees, a stipend of $8,500, and $2,000 respectively for supplies and travel are awarded each year for three years to students who enter Ph.D. or M.D.-Ph.D. programs. In 1989 there were 53 such awards.

- *Faculty Fellowships: This program provides opportunities for advanced research training to selected full-time faculty at four-year colleges, universities, and health professional schools with substantial minority enrollments. Fellows are nominated by their employing institution and may pursue the Ph.D. degree or obtain postdoctoral research training in the biomedical sciences. In 1989 there were 7 predoctoral and 5 postdoctoral awards.*

- *Visiting Scientist Program: This program provides support for periods of 3 to 12 months to outstanding scientist-teachers who serve as visiting scientists at eligible minority institutions. The intent of the program is to help strengthen research and teaching in the biomedical sciences at these institutions by allowing visiting scientists to draw on the special talents of experts.*

Statewide Mathematics Articulation

Approximately every five years, the Illinois Community College Board invites the Illinois Mathematical Association of Community Colleges and the Illinois Section of the Mathematical Association of America to form a joint task force to revise and update the Illinois Curriculum Guide for Courses in Mathematics and Computer Science in Colleges and Universities. This document contains the minimum content, range of credit hours, and suggested prerequisites for transfer-level courses in mathematics and computer science as well as pretransfer-level mathematics courses.

Each joint task force includes a mathematics faculty representative from each major state university and a like number of community college mathematics faculty representatives. The purpose of the Guide is to assist in the articulation of mathematics and computer science courses between community colleges, from any community college to any four-year college or university, and between four-year colleges and universities.

• Update this Action Plan regularly and coordinate implementation well into the next century.

Undergraduate mathematics is the linchpin of mathematics education. . . . No reform of mathematics education is possible unless it begins with revitalization of undergraduate mathematics in both curriculum and teaching style.

—Everybody Counts, 1989

MATHEMATICS BEYOND MYTHS

The United States stands at the threshold of a century that will test the national genius for scientific innovation and social adaptation. Our nation faces many urgent tasks, not least among them to revitalize undergraduate mathematics. Although the educational process is long and the pace of educational change slow, the time is ripe for reform of undergraduate mathematics. There is substantial consensus in the mathematics community on broad goals for mathematics education and on salient methods of achieving them. Professional organizations and federal agencies are supporting a variety of projects that stimulate effective change. On campuses across the nation, exemplary programs are taking root and changing the landscape of undergraduate mathematics.

The evidence from exemplary programs is clear: In mathematics, the American dream of equal educational opportunity for all need not be a myth. The dream can be achieved. We know how to do it. We know where it is being done. And we know why it must be done. The nation cannot afford to ignore this opportunity. The resources needed are not negligible, but the cost of ignoring the opportunity is incalculable. The national revitalization of mathematics is within our reach, if only we are prepared to make a serious intellectual and financial commitment to our children's and our nation's future.

SUMMARY

- Elevate the importance of undergraduate teaching.

- Engage mathematics faculty in issues of teaching and learning.

- Teach in a way that engages students.

- Achieve parity for women and minorities and the disabled.

- Establish effective career paths for college teaching.

- Broaden attitudes and value systems of the mathematics profession.

- Increase the number of students who succeed in college mathematics.

- Ensure sufficient numbers of school and college teachers.

- Elevate mathematics education to the same level as mathematical research.

- Link colleges and universities to school mathematics.

- Provide adequate resources for undergraduate mathematics.

EVIDENCE AND DOCUMENTATION

Evidence for the conclusions drawn in this report by the Committee on Mathematical Sciences in the Year 2000 was presented to the Committee in many forms, including hearings at professional meetings as well as prepared reports and testimony submitted by scientists, engineers, and mathematicians. Much of the evidence is contained in reports and studies published over the last several years. The list of references that follows includes the major reports that form the basis for the Committee's study.

Two documents [McKnight 1987, National Research Council 1989] provide documented analyses of problems concerning school mathematics and set forth key findings that serve to define issues at this educational level. The key

NCTM report [NCTM 1989] promulgates standards for curriculum and assessment in school mathematics, signalling the type of preparation that future college students may have and the type of curriculum that new teachers must be prepared to teach. The coordinated pair of recent reports [NCTM 1991, COMET 1991] establish standards for teaching school mathematics and for preparation of teachers of mathematics that are direct outgrowths of the 1989 standards document.

At the college level, two documents of the Mathematical Association of America [CUPM 1989, AAC 1990] set forth guidelines and recommendations concerning undergraduate mathematics—the first on curriculum, the second on the context of education. The 1990 document is itself heavily referenced to other reports, and includes explicit references to 68 reports and papers on undergraduate mathematics all published in the decade of the 1980s. Many of the themes raised in these two mathematics reports are reflected in a more general context in the recent Carnegie study [Boyer 1990] on the relation of scholarship to teaching.

More specialized reports have appeared on several initiatives that received much attention in recent years—improvement of calculus [Steen 1988, Tucker 1990], opportunities for enhancing college mathematics teaching [Schoenfeld 1990], the need for teaching methods that are more effective with minority students [Berriozabal 1989, Gillman 1990], improvement of graduate education [Jackson 1990], and renewal of research [BMS 1990a]. The MS2000 report [Madison 1990] outlines in great detail all relevant data concerning labor force, higher education, college and university mathematical sciences, majors in mathematics and statistics, and mathematical scientists in the workplace. Finally, the report [BMS 1990b] of the Board on Mathematical Sciences at the National Research Council suggests actions for renewal of U.S. mathematical sciences departments that are similar in many ways to the Action Plan recommended earlier in this report.

REFERENCES

Association of American Colleges Study of the Arts and Sciences Major. *Challenges for College Mathematics: An Agenda for the Next Decade.* Washington, D.C.: Mathematical Association of America, 1990.

Berriozabal, Manuel P. "Why Hasn't Mathematics Worked for Minorities?" *UME Trends,* 1:2 (May 1989) 8.

Board on Mathematical Sciences. *Renewing U.S. Mathematics: A Plan for the 1990s.* National Research Council. Washington, D.C.: National Academy Press, 1990.

Board on Mathematical Sciences. *Actions for Renewing U.S. Mathematical Sciences Departments.* Washington, D.C.: National Research Council, 1990.

Boyer, Ernest L. *Scholarship Reconsidered: Priorities of the Professoriate.* Princeton, N.J.: The Carnegie Foundation for the Advancement of Teaching, 1990.

Committee on the Mathematical Education of Teachers. *A Call for Change: Recommendations for the Mathematical Preparation of Teachers of Mathematics.* Washington, D.C.: Mathematical Association of America, 1991.

Committee on the Undergraduate Program in Mathematics. *Reshaping College Mathematics.* MAA Notes No. 13. Washington, D.C.: Mathematical Association of America, 1989.

Gillman, Leonard. "Teaching Programs That Work." *Focus,* 10:1 (1990) 7-10.

Jackson, Allyn B. "Graduate Education in Mathematics: Is it Working?" *Notices of the American Mathematical Society,* 37 (1990) 266-268.

Madison, Bernard L. and Hart, Therese A. *A Challenge of Numbers: People in the Mathematical Sciences.* Committee on Mathematical Sciences in the Year 2000, National Research Council. Washington, D.C.: National Academy Press, 1990.

McKnight, Curtis C., et al. *The Underachieving Curriculum: Assessing U.S. School Mathematics from an International Perspective.* Champaign, Ill.: Stipes Publishing Company, 1987.

National Council of Teachers of Mathematics. *Curriculum and Evaluation Standards for School Mathematics.* Reston, Va.: National Council of Teachers of Mathematics, 1989.

National Council of Teachers of Mathematics. *Professional Standards for Teaching Mathematics.* Reston, Va.: National Council of Teachers of Mathematics, 1991.

National Research Council. *Everybody Counts: A Report to the Nation on the Future of Mathematics Education.* Washington, D.C.: National Academy Press, 1989.

Schoenfeld, Alan (Ed.). *A Source Book for College Mathematics Teaching.* Washington, D.C.: Mathematical Association of America, 1990.

Steen, Lynn Arthur (Ed.). *Calculus for a New Century: A Pump, Not a Filter.* MAA Notes No. 8. Washington, D.C.: Mathematical Association of America, 1988.

Tucker, Thomas (Ed.). *Priming the Calculus Pump: Innovations and Resources.* MAA Notes No. 17. Washington, D.C.: Mathematical Association of America, 1990.

Sources

To keep the text uncluttered, it contains few reference notes concerning individuals or data. The following notes identify the sources for quotations and graphic material contained in the text.

p. 1 The quotation is from Robert M. White, president of the National Academy of Engineering, from *Calculus for a New Century*, page 9, Steen (1987).

The quotation from *Renewing U.S. Mathematics*, is from page 51, National Research Council (1990).

p. 9 The quotation from *Everybody Counts* is from page 10.

p. 13 The quotation from *Everybody Counts* is from page 41.

The quotation from *A Challenge of Numbers* is from page 4, Madison and Hart (1990).

p. 14 The quotation from *Renewing U.S. Mathematics* is from page 41.

p. 16 The quotation from *Priming the Calculus Pump* is from page 9 of Tucker (1990).

The quotation from *Renewing U.S. Mathematics* is from page 42.

p. 17 The quotation from *A Challenge of Numbers* is from page 35.

p. 19 The quotation from *A Challenge of Numbers* is from page 73.

p. 23 The quotation from *Scholarship Reconsidered: Priorities of the Professoriate* is from page 24 of Boyer (1990).

p. 25 The quotation from *Priming the Calculus Pump* is from page 9 of Tucker (1990).

p. 27 The quotation from *Renewing U.S. Mathematics* is from page 64.

p. 29 The quotation from *Challenges for College Mathematics* is from page 13 of Association of American Colleges (1990).

p. 31 The quotation from *Challenges for College Mathematics* is from page 8.

p. 43 The quotation from *Everybody Counts* is from page 39, National Research Council (1989).

Figures

Figure 1: The graph on page 32 of *A Challenge of Numbers*.

Figure 2: The graph on page 60 of *A Challenge of Numbers*.

Figure 3: The graph on page 30 of *A Challenge of Numbers*.

Figure 4: The graph on page 36 of *A Challenge of Numbers*.

Figure 5: The graph on page 36 of *A Challenge of Numbers*.

Figure 6: The graph on page 48 of *A Challenge of Numbers*.

APPENDIX

Challenges for College Mathematics:
An Agenda for the Next Decade
(Summary of Association of American Colleges–
Mathematical Association of America Report)

Goals and Objectives

- The primary goal of a mathematical sciences major should be to develop a student's capacity to undertake intellectually demanding mathematical reasoning.

- The undergraduate mathematics curriculum should be designed for all students with an interest in mathematics.

- Applications should motivate theory so that theory is seen by students as useful and enlightening.

- Mathematics majors should be offered extensive opportunities to read, write, listen, and speak mathematical ideas at each stage of their undergraduate study.

Breadth and Depth

- All students who major in mathematics should study some sequence of upper division courses that shows the power of study in depth.

- Every student who majors in mathematics should study a broad variety of advanced courses.

- Mathematics departments should take seriously the need to provide appropriate mathematical depth to students who wish to concentrate in mathematics without pursuing a traditional major.

- Mathematics majors should complete a minor in a discipline that makes significant use of mathematics.

Learning and Teaching

- Instruction should encourage students to explore mathematical ideas on their own.

- Undergraduate students should not only learn the subject of mathematics, but also learn how to learn mathematics.

- Those who teach college mathematics should seek ways to incorporate into their own teaching styles the findings of research on teaching and learning.

- Mathematicians should increase their efforts to understand better how college students learn mathematics.

- Assessment of undergraduate majors should be aligned with broad goals of the major; tests should stress what is most important, not just what is easiest to test.

- Evaluation of teaching must involve robust indicators that reflect the broad purposes of mathematics education.

Access and Encouragement

- Effective programs teach students, not just mathematics.

- National need requires greater encouragement for students to continue their study of mathematics beyond the bachelor's degree.

- To provide effective opportunities for all students to learn mathematics, colleges should offer a broader spectrum of instructional practice that is better attuned to the variety of students seeking higher education.

- To ensure for all students equal access to higher mathematics education, mathematics departments should work with nearby two-year colleges to maintain close articulation of programs.

- Smooth curricular transitions improve student learning and help maintain momentum for the study of mathematics.

Using Computers

- The mathematics curriculum should change to reflect in appropriate ways the impact of computers on the practice of mathematics.

- Colleges must recognize in budgets, staffing, and space the fact that undergraduate mathematics is rapidly becoming a laboratory discipline.

Doing Mathematics

- Dealing with open-ended problem situations should be one of the highest priorities of undergraduate mathematics.

- All undergraduate mathematics students should undertake open-ended projects whose scope extends well beyond typical textbook problems.

- Undergraduate research and senior projects should be encouraged wherever there is sufficient faculty to provide appropriate supervision.

- Students majoring in mathematics should undertake some real-world mathematical modelling project.

Students

- Building students' well-founded self-confidence should be a major priority for all undergraduate mathematics instruction.
- Careful and individualized advising is crucial to students' success.
- All mathematics students should engage in serious study of the historical context and contemporary impact of mathematics.
- Mathematics departments should actively encourage extracurricular programs that enhance peer group support among mathematics majors.

Renewal

- It is important for mathematics departments to help faculty and students recognize their own perspectives on mathematics and understand the perspectives of others.
- To ensure continued vitality of undergraduate mathematics programs, all mathematics faculty should engage in public professional activity, broadly defined.
- Regular external reviews and informal feedback are needed to assure quality in departments of mathematics.
- Renewal of undergraduate mathematics will require commitment, leadership, and support of graduate schools.

COMMITTEE ON THE MATHEMATICAL SCIENCES IN THE YEAR 2000

William E. Kirwan (Chairman), President, University of Maryland at College Park

Ramesh A. Gangolli (Vice Chairman), Professor of Mathematics, University of Washington

Lida K. Barrett, Past President, Mathematical Association of America, Dean, College of Arts and Sciences, Mississippi State University

Maria A. Berriozabal, Councilwoman, City of San Antonio, Texas

Ernest L. Boyer, President, Carnegie Foundation for the Advancement of Teaching, New Jersey

William Browder, Professor of Mathematics, Princeton University, New Jersey

Rita R. Colwell, Director, Maryland Biotechnology Institute, Professor of Microbiology, University of Maryland

John M. Deutch, Professor of Chemistry, Massachusetts Institute of Technology

Ronald G. Douglas, Vice Provost for Academic Affairs, State University of New York, Stony Brook

Patricia A. Dyer, Vice President for Academic Affairs, Palm Beach Community College, Florida

Lloyd C. Elam, Distinguished Service Professor of Psychiatry, Meharry Medical College, Tennessee

Sheldon L. Glashow, Higgins Professor of Physics, Harvard University, Massachusetts

Nancy J. Kopell, Professor of Mathematics, Boston University, Massachusetts

Donald W. Marquardt, Consultant Manager, E.I. du Pont de Nemours and Co., Delaware

David S. Moore, Professor of Statistics, Purdue University, Indiana

Jaime Oaxaca, Vice Chairman, Coronado Communications, Inc., California

Moshe F. Rubinstein, Professor of Engineering and Applied Science, University of California, Los Angeles

Ivar Stakgold, Chairman, Department of Mathematical Sciences, University of Delaware

S. Frederick Starr, President, Oberlin College, Ohio

Lynn Arthur Steen, Professor of Mathematics, St. Olaf College, Minnesota

Staff

Bernard L. Madison, Project Director through December 1989

James A. Voytuk, Project Director

BOARD ON MATHEMATICAL SCIENCES

Joseph W. Duncan, Corporate Vice President and Chief Economist, The Dun & Bradstreet Corporation, New York

Wade Ellis, Jr., Mathematics Instructor, West Valley College, California

Ramanathan Gnanadesikan, Assistant Vice President, Mathematical, Communication & Computer Sciences Research Laboratory, Bell Communications Research, New Jersey

Jackie Goldberg, President, Board of Education, Los Angeles Unified School District, California

Norbert S. Hill, Jr., Executive Director, American Indian Science and Engineering Society, Colorado

Harvey Keynes, Professor of Mathematics, Director, Minnesota Mathematics Mobilization, University of Minnesota

Richard S. Lindzen, Sloan Professor of Meteorology, Massachusetts Institute of Technology

Ruth McMullin, Past President, John Wiley & Sons, Westport, Connecticut

Steven P. Meiring, Mathematics Specialist, Ohio State Department of Education

Jose P. Mestre, Associate Professor of Physics, University of Massachusetts

Calvin C. Moore, Associate Vice President, Academic Affairs, University of California, Berkeley

Jo Ann Mosier, Mathematics Teacher, Fairdale High School, Kentucky

Robert Nielsen, Assistant to the President for Higher Education, American Federation of Teachers, Washington, D.C.

Leslie Hiles Paoletti, Chairman, Mathematics and Computer Science, Choate Rosemary Hall, Connecticut

Isadore M. Singer, Institute Professor, Massachusetts Institute of Technology

Lynn Arthur Steen, Professor of Mathematics, St. Olaf College, Minnesota

William P. Thurston, Professor of Mathematics, Princeton University, New Jersey

John S. Toll, President, Universities Research Association, Inc., Washington, D.C., Chancellor Emeritus and Professor of Physics, University of Maryland

P. Uri Treisman, Director, Charles A. Dana Center for Mathematics and Science Education, University of California, Berkeley

Manya S. Ungar, Past President, National Parents and Teachers Association, Scotch Plains, New Jersey

Zalman Usiskin, Director, School Mathematics Project, Professor of Education, University of Chicago

John B. Walsh, Vice President, Research and Engineering Programs, Boeing Aerospace and Electronics, Washington

Larry D. Williams, Chairman, Department of Mathematics, Eutaw High School, Alabama

James J. Wynne, Manager, Biological and Molecular Science, IBM Thomas J. Watson Research Center, New York

Staff

Kenneth M. Hoffman, Executive Director through February 1991

Ray C. Shiflett, Executive Director

Michael H. Clapp, Associate Executive Director

CREDITS FOR MOVING BEYOND MYTHS

AMERICAN MATHEMATICAL SOCIETY

Janene Winter, Composition
Ralph Youngen, Composition
Julie Wilczek, Composition

NATIONAL ACADEMY PRESS

Francesca Moghari, Cover Design
Susan England, Graphic Design
James Butler, Graphics
Dorothy Lewis, Production
Carla McCullough, Production

MATHEMATICAL SCIENCES EDUCATION BOARD

Michael Clapp, Associate Executive Director
Linda Rosen, Associate Director for Policy Studies

COMPOSITION COURTESY OF

American Mathematical Society

FINANCIAL SUPPORT

We also wish to thank the National Science Foundation and the National Security Agency for their generous support and the Department of Education and the National Aeronautics and Space Administration for additional support.